Anonymous

Words From Many Sources Commendatory of Its Work

And especially of the plan to purchase the house in which President

Lincoln died

Anonymous

Words From Many Sources Commendatory of Its Work
And especially of the plan to purchase the house in which President Lincoln died

ISBN/EAN: 9783337403508

Printed in Europe, USA, Canada, Australia, Japan

Cover: Foto ©ninafisch / pixelio.de

More available books at **www.hansebooks.com**

The Memorial Association

OF THE DISTRICT OF COLUMBIA.

⚹⚹

Words from many sources commendatory of its work; and especially of the plan to purchase the house in which President Lincoln died.

The Memorial Association

OF THE DISTRICT OF COLUMBIA.

Incorporated under the Laws of the District, March 18, 1892.

This Association has been organized for the threefold purpose—

1. Of preserving the most noteworthy houses at the Capital that have been made historic by the residence of the nation's greatest men.

2. Of suitably marking, by tablets or otherwise, the houses and places throughout the city of chief interest to our own residents and to the multitudes of Americans and foreigners who annually visit the Capital.

3. Of thus cultivating that historic spirit and that reverence for the memories of the founders and leaders of the Republic upon which an intelligent and abiding patriotism so largely depends.

Officers of the Association.

MELVILLE W. FULLER, *President.*	MYRON M. PARKER, *Secretary.*
TEUNIS S. HAMLIN, *Vice-President.*	JAMES E. FITCH, *Treasurer.*

Members of the Association,

APPOINTED BY THE PRESIDENT OF THE UNITED STATES, THE PRESIDENT OF THE SENATE, AND THE SPEAKER OF THE HOUSE.

MELVILLE W. FULLER.	J. C. BANCROFT DAVIS.	MYRON M. PARKER.
JOHN M. SCHOFIELD.	WALTER S. COX.	GARDINER G. HUBBARD.
JOHN W. FOSTER.	S. H. KAUFFMANN.	W. D. DAVIDGE.
B. H. WARDER.	A. R. SPOFFORD.	S. R. FRANKLIN.
S. P. LANGLEY.	JOHN HAY.	CHARLES C. GLOVER.
A. B. HAGNER.	J. W. DOUGLASS.	TEUNIS S. HAMLIN.

TABLE OF CONTENTS.

OFFICIAL PERSONAGES.

GOVERNORS OF STATES.

Hon. WM. M. FISHBACK, .	Arkansas
Hon. DAVIS H. WAITE, .	Colorado
Hon. ROBERT J REYNOLDS, .	Delaware
Hon. WILLIAM J. McCONNELL,	. Idaho
Hon. JOHN P. ALTGELD, . .	. Illinois
Hon CLAUDE MATTHEWS,	Indiana
Hon. WILLIAM E. RUSSELL,	. Mass.
Hon. JOHN T. RICH, . . .	Michigan
Hon. J. E. RICHARDS, .	Montana
Hon. WILLIAM J. STONE,	Missouri
Hon. L. CROUNSE, . .	Nebraska
Hon. JOHN B. SMITH, . .	New Hampshire
Hon. ROSWELL K. COLCORD,	. Nevada
Hon. ROSWELL P. FLOWER . .	New York
Hon. WILLIAM McKINLEY, Jr.	. . Ohio
Hon. ROBERT E. PATTISON, .	. . Penn.
Hon. T. P. TILLMAN, . .	. S. Carolina
Hon. D. RUSSELL BROWN, .	Rhode Island
Hon. JOHN S. HOGG. . .	. Texas
Hon. LEVI K. FULLER,	. Vermont
Hon. JOHN H. McGRAW, .	Washington
Hon. WILLIAM A. McCORKLE,	. West Va.
Hon. JOHN E. OSBORNE, .	Wyoming

CLERGYMEN. EDUCATORS AND OTHERS.

California.

BISHOP NICHOLS
DAVID S. JORDAN,
     President Leland Stanford, Junior, University.

CHARLES J. SWIFT.

Connecticut.

BISHOP WILLIAMS.

5

Delaware.

BISHOP COLEMAN.
JAMES P. WINCHESTER.
　　President First National Bank, Wilmington.

Colorado.

BISHOP WARREN.
DONALD FLETCHER (Denver).

District of Columbia.

BISHOP HURST.
BISHOP KEANE.
FREDERICK DOUGLASS.
J. E. RANKIN, D. D.,
　　President Howard University.

B. H. WARNER,
　　President Washington Loan and Trust Co.

Newspapers.

DAILY POST.
EVENING STAR.

Georgia.

BISHOP NELSON.
BISHOP HAYGOOD.

Illinois.

BISHOP MERRILL.
JOHN HENRY BARROWS, D. D.
HERRICK JOHNSON, D. D.
Hon. E. S. LACEY,
　　Late Comptroller of the Currency.

Iowa.

BISHOP PERRY.
O. L. F. BROWN, Esq.,
　　Secretary Commercial Exchange, Des Moines.

Indiana.

BISHOP KNICKERBACKER,

6

Newspapers.
INDIANAPOLIS JOURNAL.

Kansas.

E. N. MORRILL,
President First National Bank, Leavenworth.

Newspapers.
WYANDOTTE HERALD,
KANSAS CITY JOURNAL.

Kentucky.

T. T. EATON, D. D.
BISHOP DUDLEY.

Louisiana.

N. BALDWIN,
President N. O. National Bank.

Newspapers.
PICAYUNE (NEW ORLEANS).
TIMES-DEMOCRAT (NEW ORLEANS).

Maine.

WILLIAM DE W. HYDE,
President Bowdoin College.
HON. CHARLES F. LIBBY,
President Maine Bar Association.

Newspapers.
KENNEBEC JOURNAL.

Massachusetts.

A. J. GORDON, D. D. (BOSTON).
BISHOP LAWRENCE.
MERRILL E. GATES,
President Amherst College.
JUSTIN WINSOR, (CAMBRIDGE).
ALBERT CLARKE,
Secretary Home Market Club, Boston.
DR. O. W. HOLMES (BOSTON).

Newspapers.
THE DAILY GLOBE (Boston).
THE DAILY TRANSCRIPT (Boston).
THE DAILY TRAVELLER (Boston).
THE CONGREGATIONALIST (Boston).

Maryland.

CARDINAL GIBBONS.
F. M ELLIS, D. D. (Baltimore).
BISHOP PARET,
D. C. GILMAN,
        Johns Hopkins.
JOSEPH PACKARD.

Newspapers

BALTIMORE NEWS.
BALTIMORE SUN.

Michigan.

BISHOP DAVIS.
BISHOP NINDE.
JAMES B. ANGELL,
        President University of Michigan.

Minnesota.

BISHOP WHIPPLE.
BISHOP FOWLER.
CYRUS NORTHROP,
        President University of Minnesota.
CHARLES E. FLANDRAU.

Missouri.

F. A. McWILLIE.
BISHOP LUTTLE.
BISHOP BOWMAN.
R. H. JESSE,
        President University of Missouri.

Nebraska.

THE DAILY BEE (Omaha).
THE WORLD-HERALD (Omaha).

New Hampshire.

WILLIAM J. TUCKER,
President Dartmouth College.

New Jersey.

BISHOP SCARBOROUGH.

Newspapers.
THE CHRONICLE (Orange).

New York.

LYMAN ABBOTT, D. D.
MORGAN DIX, D. D.
ROBERT COLLYER.
CHARLES H. PARKHURST, D. D.
THOMAS A. HASTINGS, D. D.,
Union Theological Seminary.

R. S. McARTHUR, D. D
PHILLIP SCHAFF, D. D.
JOHN HALL, D. D.
BISHOP POTTER.
BISHOP FITZGERALD.
BISHOP LITTLEJOHN (Long Island).
BISHOP VINCENT.
BISHOP HUNTINGTON.
BISHOP MALLALIEU (Buffalo).
J. G. SCHURMAN,
President Cornell University.
Hon. J. NEWTON FIERO,
President New York Bar Association.
C. N. SIMS,
Syracuse University.
ALEXANDER WEBB,
College of the City of New York.

GEORGE CLINTON,
President Mercantile Exchange, Buffalo
H. H. McCRACKEN,
University of the City of New York.
JOHN CROSBY BROWN.
WILLIAM E. DODGE.

Newspapers.
DAILY TRIBUNE (NEW YORK)
DAILY MAIL AND EXPRESS (NEW YORK).
ALBANY EVENING JOURNAL.

Ohio.
ARCHBISHOP ELDER.
BISHOP LEONARD.
WILLIAM G. BALLANTYNE,
President Oberlin College.
WILLIAM C. SPROUL,
Dean University of Cincinnati.
SYLVESTER F. SCOVEL,
President of the University of Wooster.

Newspapers.
COMMERCIAL-GAZETTE (CINCINNATI).

Pennsylvania.
GEORGE DANA BOARDMAN, D. D., PH. D.
I. D. MOFFAT,
President Washington and Jefferson College.

Newspapers.
THE TIMES (PITTSBURGH).

Rhode Island.
BISHOP CLARK,
E. BENJAMIN ANDREWS,
Brown University.

South Carolina.
CHARLES S VEDDER, D. D (CHARLESTON).
B. F. WHITNER,
President Bar Association of S. C.
JAMES WOODWARD,
President South Carolina College.

Tennessee.

BISHOP QUINTARD.

Texas.

BISHOP GARRETT.

Newspapers.

THE DAILY POST (Houston).

Wisconsin.

ARCHBISHOP KATZER (Milwaukee).
C. K. ADAMS,
    President University of Wisconsin.

Vermont.

Newspapers.

THE FREE PRESS (Burlington.)

Virginia.

J. C. GRANBERRY.
R. S. BARTON (Winchester).

Newspapers.

THE JEFFERSONIAN (Piedmont).

West Virginia.

THE STATE JOURNAL (Parkersburg).

The Memorial Association

From Vice-President A. E. STEVENSON:

"I need hardly assure you that I am in full sympathy with the action outlined by the Memorial Association. The plan you suggest of purchasing the house in which President Lincoln died meets with my heartiest approval. I trust early and favorable action looking to that end will be taken by Congress."

From Ex-Vice-President LEVI P. MORTON:

"I am in hearty sympathy with the disinterested and public-spirited purposes of the Memorial Association, and look forward with confidence to an appropriation by Congress at its next session for the purchase of the house in which President Lincoln died."

From W. H. H. MILLER, Ex-Attorney General:

"The purpose of the Memorial Association is most commendable. The places associated with memorable events where heroic actions have been performed, where the world's really great and good men have lived and died, have associations full of inspiration. To mark such places and preserve their hallowed memories is to render a service to the country and to posterity of inestimable value. Your work deserves, and I trust will receive, public favor."

From JOHN W. NOBLE, Ex-Secretary of the Interior :

" The work proposed to be done by the Memorial Association is most worthy and patriotic and cannot but add many important facts to history and increase greatly the interest we all feel in the city of Washington."

From the Hon. ROBERT C. WINTHROP, of Massachusetts :

" The Memorial Association of the District of Columbia is engaged in a most interesting work, and is entitled to the sympathy and support of all patriotic citizens."

From the Hon. ABRAM S. HEWITT, of New York :

" I think that your effort is most commendable, and I shall be very glad, indeed, to learn that the house where President Lincoln died has become public property, so that our descendants may resort to it for patriotic inspiration."

From the late CARTER H. HARRISON, Mayor of Chicago :

" I am in receipt of your favor of September 27th, relative to the Congressional appropriation for the purchase of the house in which President Lincoln died.

" I cheerfully commend the movement inaugurated by your Association, and hope the project will be consummated speedily.

" Such spots, even though they mark the saddest events in our history, should be kept sacred for all time."

From the Hon. ANDREW D. WHITE, Ex-President of Cornell University, and late Minister to Germany, and now Minister to Russia :

" All the things planned seem to me exceedingly valuable, but the proposal to urge upon Congress the purchase of the house in which Abraham Lincoln died strikes me as perhaps the best part of your plan. Should that be done it would be a place of pilgrimage from all parts of the world and for many centuries."

From the Hon. THOMAS M. COOLEY, Ex-Chairman of the Interstate Commerce Commission :

" I approve fully of the purposes for which the Memorial Association of the District of Columbia is organized, and shall be glad to see them given effect."

From the Hon. HENRY L. DAWES, Ex-Senator from Massachusetts:

" I am glad to see the earnestness with which your society has entered upon this work, and hope from its researches rich results."

From Mr. JOHN CROSBY BROWN, of New York:

" The object the Association has in view speaks for itself and commends itself to all good citizens. If I can be of any service to you I shall be most happy."

From the Hon. WILLIAM E. DODGE, of New York:

I am greatly interested in the patriotic and wise plans of your Memorial Association. Nothing could be more helpful than to keep constantly before the country the mementoes of the great and good men who have made our nation famous and given us a permanent and stable Government. The remembrance of the life and work of our great men will always be an inspiration to those who are coming on to fill their places."

From the Hon. WM. WALTER PHELPS, late Minister to Germany:

"As I just now read the purpose for which you had associated yourselves—the care for local association and the preservation of the old and famous in our streets—I said, 'My interest in such things was apologetic and timid, because I did not expect sympathy; and here are about all the prominent men I know in Washington, who not only care for such things, but have begun to work for them.' You may imagine, then, the ardor with which I hailed the mission of the Memorial Association."

From Mr. JUSTIN WINSOR, the historian, of Cambridge, Mass. :

"The work the Association proposes is every way commendable, and in it the patriotic and historic sense are united in ends serviceable to the moral and even material well-being of our people."

From Dr. OLIVER WENDELL HOLMES, of Boston :

"I heartily sympathize with the Memorial Association in its proposed efforts to secure for posterity those buildings and monuments which are associated with the memory of the great citizens of the Republic. Boston allowed the Hancock House to be torn to pieces and sold for fire-wood, to the great grief of many good Bostonians, but she keeps Faneuil Hall and the old State House. She would not know herself without them. I hope Washington will look to us for a warning and an example."

From the Hon. FREDERICK DOUGLASS, of Washington:

" The idea of preserving intact the house in which Abraham Lincoln, our martyred President, died is worthy of your action.

" Nothing, is too costly, either of money or of effort, which tends to keep in memory the man by whose wisdom and beneficence the Union of our country was saved and the emancipation of millions secured. I am glad to see that the measure you contemplate is in worthy and able hands, and I have no doubt it will be carried into effect."

From Mr. JOSEPH PACKARD, Jr., of Baltimore:

" It seems to me that it is both proper and timely to take such action as your Association proposes. Nowhere can it be more fitting to preserve the memorials of the past than in the city of Washington, which touches so closely the history of our Federal Government—a history which will draw deepening interest as our country grows and prospers. I may add that your project has a peculiar interest for citizens of the State of Maryland, which ceded from her domain the territory which constitutes the District as it now exists, and whose citizens were prominent among the founders of the federal city."

From Mr. J. C. GRANBERY, of Ashland, Virginia :

"I heartily approve the wise and patriotic purposes of the Memorial Association, and trust that it will meet with popular favor."

FROM GOVERNORS OF STATES.

From the Hon. WILLIAM M. FISHBACK, Governor of Arkansas :

"I regard your Association as a highly meritorious institution. Its aims are at once patriotic, historic, and public spirited, and as such should be encouraged by Congress."

From the Hon. DAVIS H. WAITE, Governor of Colorado :

"I take it the good that comes from your labors will not be so much in the collection and preservation of the mere material things which have belonged to great men as in the association of those things with that clear conception of right which has made great men really great. I hope your Association will be of great service in cultivating clear conceptions of human rights."

18

From the Hon. ROBERT J. REYNOLDS, Governor of Delaware :

" I certainly regard the aim and purpose of the Memorial Association a commendable one, and no reasonable outlay of time or money I consider too great to make your undertaking a success and a permanent one."

From the Hon. WILLIAM J. McCONNELL, Governor of Idaho :

" The organization of such an association was a happy thought, and the fact that you have enlisted in it such names as appear on your roll of officers and members is a guarantee of the faithfulness with which the work in hand will be prosecuted.

" The preservation of those buildings which have connected with them so many memories and associations inclined to inspire the patriotism not only of the present generation, but of generations yet unborn, should, and no doubt will, receive the approval and support of Congress at its next session. The appropriation needed will be very small in comparison with the universal interest which the subject will command. I think I may congratulate you in advance upon the success of your very commendable enterprise."

From the Hon. JOHN P. ALTGELD, Governor of Illinois :

" The Memorial Association has my hearty approval and good wishes. The rescuing of the buildings that were associated with the memory of many of our great men is not only patriotic, but is a work which this age owes to posterity."

From the HON. CLAUDE MATTHEWS, Governor of Indiana :

"The object of your Association impresses me as one meriting encouragement from all. To preserve the historical features of Washington, now fast being obliterated or passing into decay, that they may present lessons to the youth of our country is certainly a noble and high purpose. I trust you may meet with every encouragement that will insure the success of your undertaking."

From the HON. WILLIAM E. RUSSELL, Governor of Massachusetts :

"I have read with much interest the statement of your Memorial Association. It seems to me its purposes are most commendable and patriotic, and I heartly wish for it every success."

From the HON. JOHN T. RICH, Governor of Michigan :

"The work you are doing is an important one for the American people, especially for the generation yet to come, and I hope Congress will give you such substantial aid as the cause for which you are at work merits."

From the Hon. J. E. RICHARDS, Governor
of Montana:

" In no better way can a spirit of patriotism be
fostered and the great deeds of the heroic dead
indelibly impressed upon the public mind. An appropriation to purchase the house in which Lincoln
died would, I believe, meet the hearty endorsement
of all who treasure the memory of the great libera-
tor."

From the Hon. WILLIAM J. STONE, Governor of Missouri:

" I beg to express my warm approval of the
effort your Association is making to excite a greater
interest among our people in those things defined
by you as representing " the higher refinements of a
splendid civilization." It is painfully true that we
pay too little attention to art, literature, and the
like. We have not sufficiently cultivated the gen-
tler graces of civilization. I agree with you that
' among those refinements none is more precious
than that worthy pride in our best national traits
and achievements,' and that that pride is best stim-
ulated by an intimate acquaintance with the life
and work of our greatest men. So believing, I can
only wish that your efforts may be crowned with
the largest measure of success."

From the Hon. L. CROUNSE, Governor of Nebraska:

"The work in which your Association is engaged, in rescuing and preserving those landmarks of American history, which must be so interesting and valuable in time to come, is most praiseworthy and deserving of every encouragement."

From the Hon. JOHN B. SMITH, Governor of New Hampshire:

"Your aims and purposes are, indeed, commendable. These old landmarks and historic homes and buildings at the nation's capital are interesting to the people of the whole country, especially any house identified with Abraham Lincoln, who, to-day, is in the hearts of all loyal people of the land more than any other man of this century."

From the Hon. ROSWELL K. COLCORD, Governor of Nevada:

"The objects for which your Association was organized are most worthy, and will meet the highest commendation of all true Americans. You have undertaken a noble and patriotic work, in which the whole nation is deeply interested, and will pray that you may receive all necessary aid from Congress. I hereby extend to you my very best wishes for the success of the enterprise."

From the Hon. ROSWELL P. FLOWER, Governor of New York :

" I wish your Association great success in its efforts to preserve the historic buildings and landmarks of Washington. The capital of our country is dear to every American, and its historic associations and traditions should be carefully cherished. I congratulate you on the good work that has already been accomplished by your Association, and hope that success will continue to crown your efforts."

From the Hon. WILLIAM McKINLEY, Jr., Governor of Ohio :

" I take great pleasure in commending the work of your Association. It appeals to the patriotism and historic pride of all Americans, and I sincerely trust that Congress can be interested in the matter."

From the Hon. ROBERT E. PATTISON, Governor of Pennsylvania :

" I am pleased to express to you my commendation of the work upon which the Association has entered, and sincerely hope that nothing may intervene to prevent an early realization of all that is anticipated by the patriotic and progressive men who have been enlisted in this good work."

From the Hon. T. P. TILLMAN, Governor of South Carolina :

"Permit me to say that I think the purpose of your organization an admirable one, and that you will deserve the thanks of the present and all future generations if you shall succeed in carrying out that purpose."

From the Hon. D. RUSSELL BROWN, Governor of Rhode Island :

"The work of preserving and marking historic houses and spots is a most laudable one, although up to the present time greatly neglected, and it must be a matter of gratification to those who sympathize with it to find so many persons of experience and prominence engaged in the undertaking. Any assistance I can render in my humble way will be given with much pleasure."

From the Hon. J. S. HOGG, Governor of Texas :

"I beg to express my best wishes for the success of your efforts in taking care of and suitably marking the most noteworthy houses and places at the capital that have been made historic by the residence of the nation's greatest men. Your patriotic motive will, I feel sure, win success."

From the Hon. LEVI K. FULLER, Governor
of Vermont:

" I need not say that your object is a worthy one,
nor that I am heartily in sympathy with all movements looking to the care and preservation of historic houses, etc., in our country. Places associated
with the lives of those who have in a greater or
less degree helped to make our nation what it is
to-day are and must continue to be sources of inspiration to the young and rising generation. I
therefore trust that the work of your Association
may long be successfully prosecuted."

From the Hon. JOHN H. McGRAW, Governor of Washington:

" The object of your organization is most commendable, and should receive substantial assistance
from Congress. Anything that tends to awaken
and propagate the spirit of patriotism in our people
should be cherished and fostered."

From the Hon. WILLIAM A. McCORKLE,
Governor of West Virginia:

" I view with pleasure the work which you have
undertaken, and deem it one which commends itself to every patriotic American. It is a duty
which we owe to future generations to preserve for
them the historic places of the first century's
growth of the greatest government the world has
ever known."

From the Hox. JOHN E. OSBORNE, Governor of Wyoming:

"I am greatly pleased with the designs proposed. The object is certainly a worthy one, and I sincerely hope you will be able to secure the appropriation you seek."

FROM COLLEGE PRESIDENTS.

From D. C. GILMAN, of Johns Hopkins University:

"I have not the slightest hesitation in commending the plans of your society. The name of your president, the Chief Justice of the United States, the ability of your associates, and the clear statement of the object you have in view, afford ample assurance of success. You have a capital idea, supported by the best citizens of Washington, and you will doubtless produce such an impression that other cities throughout the land will follow your example. Washington has already become one of the most attractive capitals of the world. A slight flavor of antiquity will be no disadvantage."

From WILLIAM O. SPROUL, Dean of the University of Cincinnati:

"I heartily approve of the object of the Memorial Association, and should like to see similar organizations (perhaps as branches) established elsewhere. It inspires the people with love of country, and warms them to deeds of patriotism to see, to touch and to handle, objects that pertain to the daily life of our great men, or which are closely connected with our country's history."

From H. M. McCRACKEN, Chancellor of the University of the City of New York :

" I most heartily applaud the aims of your association. Having made many a pilgrimage in foreign cities to find houses made famous by great men who have dwelt in them, I have felt grateful to those who have preserved them. I am sure that large benefits may be conferred on all the generations that shall visit Washington by directing their steps to the homes of the men who have dwelt there. I wish you the largest success in your work."

From E. BENJAMIN ANDREWS, President of Brown University, Providence, Rhode Island :

" Your plan seems to me a most excellent one, and I can have no doubt that it will effect the ends for which it has been devised."

From FRANKLIN CARTER, President of Williams College :

" The purposes of the Memorial Association commend themselves warmly to an American who has pride in the history of the nation, and it seems to me nothing could be better suited to develop patriotism and reverence than the attainment of these endeavors. I earnestly hope that this feeling will be general, and that the society will not find it difficult to carry these purposes into effect."

From JAMES B. ANGELL, President of the University of Michigan :

" It is with great interest that I have read the announcement of the project of the Memorial Association. The traveller in Europe finds many of the sites and the houses which have been made memorable by the lives of great men set apart and preserved with care. It is high time that we began to imitate their example. I have been especially struck with the need in Washington of the work you are undertaking, as I have sought often in vain to learn where some of our most eminent statesmen dwelt in that city. It is a pious and patriotic duty which you are discharging, and I wish you all success in it."

From ALEXANDER S. WEBB, President of the College of the City of New York :

" I cannot refrain from writing in commendation of your work in preserving the most noteworthy houses at the capital made historic by the residence of the nation's greatest men. Yes, cultivate reverence for such memories."

From MERRILL E. GATES, President of Amherst College :

" The awakening and deepening of historic consciousness tends always and directly to the deepening and intensifying of patriotism. I sincerely hope that the objects of the Memorial Association will be accomplished. The work should command the cordial support of all public-spirited citizens."

From C. K. ADAMS, President of the University of Wisconsin :

" I approve entirely of your scheme. Every effort to preserve buildings of historical importance ought to receive the encouragement of every person having any interest in history."

From JAMES WOODROW, President of the South Carolina College :

" I wish your Association the highest success in the accomplishment of every part of your three-fold purpose."

From DAVID S. JORDAN, President of the Leland Stanford, Junior, University :

" I wish to express my entire sympathy with the purposes of the Memorial Association, and I sincerely hope that you may be able to secure the funds necessary for the purchase of the house in which Lincoln died."

From WILLIAM J. TUCKER, President of Dartmouth College :

"The value of the work which you have taken in hand cannot be overestimated. And it is timely. The memorials which you seek to preserve can now be secured, and they have already become historic. It does not seem possible that your appeal to the loyal citizens of the country can fail."

From WILLIAM DEW. HYDE, President of Bowdoin College :

"I thank you for calling my attention to the effort of the Memorial Association. It is a most praiseworthy undertaking, and both in your general purpose and also in your immediate endeavor to secure the house in which President Lincoln died I wish you success."

From WILLIAM G. BALLANTINE, President of Oberlin College :

"I am gratified to learn of the organization and purposes of the Memorial Association. Its work is one of which every true patriot must heartily approve."

From CYRUS NORTHROP, President of the University of Minnesota :

"The Memorial Association seems to me to have a very noble purpose, and I hope it may be very

successful. Our country is especially lacking in
places of old, historic interest, and it is very desirable that objects of historic interest should be preserved if possible."

From R. H. JESSE, President of the University of Missouri :

" I am in cordial sympathy with the aims of the
Association, and wish you Godspeed in your
work."

From J. G. SCHURMAN, President of Cornell
University :

" Civilization means, above all things, a sense of
the historic past ; and I know of nothing more
important for our American civilization than that
the names of our great men should be held in
reverent and intelligent remembrance. As a means
to this end the preservation and marking of the
houses in which our heroes lived is a most important
undertaking, and I wish the Memorial Association
all the success which its high object deserves."

From C. N. SIMS, late Chancellor of the
Syracuse University :

" I most heartily approve the objects of your
organization. The day will come when the nation
will hold as priceless the historic buildings which
your Association proposes to own and protect, and
the tablets by which it may commemorate events
of historic interest."

From J. D. MOFFAT, President of Washington and Jefferson College :

" Your good work has begun none too soon. Places associated with the lives and services of our great statesmen, warriors, and leaders become in time one of the most effective agencies for the cultivation of patriotism—a virtue that is apt to disappear with excessive pursuit of wealth, unless kept alive by historic places and celebrations. I trust you will be successful in this new enterprise."

From SYLVESTER F. SCOVEL, President of the University of Wooster :

" I am delighted to find that this new method at once of awakening and gratifying an interest in our national past has been thought of and has been committed to such able custody and undertaken in so thoroughly a disinterested way. I sincerely trust you will not only secure all the official appropriations necessary, but be sustained and cheered in your noble work by a most uniform and pronounced sympathy from all who are thoughtful enough thoroughly to appreciate how vital a nation's history is to its nobler future, and how essentially the biography of that history will contain some of its most striking elements, and how surely locality is connected with biography."

From J. E. RANKIN, President of Howard University:

"Anything that can be done by Americans to make memorial things sacred to their children ought to be done. We are an irreverent people, and we so emphasize the present that the past has little charm for us. While the truth is, unless a nation takes care of its past, it soon neglects its future. I am heartily in sympathy with the Memorial Association."

FROM EMINENT CLERGYMEN.

From CARDINAL GIBBONS:

" The three-fold purpose for which your Association has been organized is worthy of the highest commendation. Our patriotism and love of country should be second only to our devotion to and love of God; and it seems to me an Association whose chief care is to preserve and to call constant attention to the houses and places where the founders and leaders of our glorious Republic have lived and moved is well calculated to inspire these sentiments."

From BISHOP KEANE, Rector of the Catholic University:

(At the opening of the Lincoln House.) " The longer I live and the more I love America, the more I thank God for the example of Lincoln. The work of consecrating this edifice to his memory is a noble one. We have not much history in this country of ours, but, brief as it is, it is high and worth preserving. May God bless this work, in which I pledge my heartiest co-operation."

From ARCHBISHOP ELDER, of Cincinnati :

" Your work of preserving and making permanent the houses and places associated with the memory of those who have been benefactors of their country is one efficacious means of perpetuating this wholesome remembrance of the men and women of whom we have reason to be proud. It will be well if the example of your association at the capital of the country give an impulse to similar movements elsewhere."

From ARCHBISHOP KATZER, of Milwaukee :

" I consider the object of your Association a most happy and patriotic idea, which is in every way commendable, and deserving the support of the citizens of this great Republic."

From ARCHBISHOP GROSS, of Oregon :

" Having visited Rome, London and Paris, and so many other capital cities of Europe, I can well testify to the care which is everywhere taken of preserving the noteworthy houses, and of suitably marking by tablets the houses and places of noble memory elsewhere. I heartily approve the project of similarly distinguishing the places and houses of historic interest in the capital city of our country. Nothing, in my opinion, will better serve to promote that reverence and love for our native land, and her glorious Constitution and liberties, than these silent memories of departed heroes and patriots. I heartily wish the Memorial Association eminent success."

From JOHN HENRY BARROWS, D. D., of Chicago :

"The objects proposed by your Association meet my hearty and enthusiastic approval. Every patriotic American will be grateful if you succeed in preserving the historic houses of the nation's capital, and of marking with tablets the places of historic interest in Washington. The spirit which you will thus quicken and deepen is the spirit essential to the highest well-being of the Republic."

From LYMAN ABBOTT, D. D., of Brooklyn :

"I am most heartily in sympathy with the plans and purposes of the Memorial Association. I hope it may achieve such success that similar organizations may be started in other parts of the country for the purpose of preserving memorials of historic interest, which are now far too readily destroyed, as though they were of no value."

From MORGAN DIX, D. D., Rector of Trinity P. E. Church, New York:

"The design of procuring from Congress an appropriation for the purchase of the house in which President Lincoln died meets my approval. I think it of great importance that historic relics of this class should be preserved, and I trust that you will meet with good success in the prosecution of your design. The plan of marking notable houses in the city of New York with notable tablets, or designating in such manner the spots at which important events have occurred, is one which has been undertaken, and is now successfully prosecuted, by the Society of the Sons of the Revolution. We have already done some very good work in this line and have much more in prospect."

From ROBERT COLLYER, of New York:

" It is a good thing you propose to do in the purchase of the house in which President Lincoln died, and I think the nation will be with you in sympathy and the means."

From CHARLES H. PARKHURST, D. D, of New York:

" I am so warmly in sympathy with everything that the Association represents that I would love to give it the support of my presence as well as of my word." (In reply to an invitation to attend the opening of the Lincoln House.)

From HERRICK JOHNSON, D. D., of Chicago :

"A most beautiful memorial purpose, beneficent to the living and reverent to the dead, perpetuating that which is best in historic scene and association, and stimulative to all loyal hearts."

From T. T. EATON, D. D., Editor of the *Western Recorder*, Louisville, Kentucky :

"The movement has my hearty sympathy, and I take occasion to commend it in this week's *Recorder*."

From R. S. McARTHUR, D. D., of New York :

"I am in hearty sympathy with the object and aim of this organization. We have neglected too much to cultivate the historic spirit. If we do not adopt some practical measures now, in a few years these places will have faded from the memory of our people, and the young of our land will be ignorant of the great national events to which these places bear witness. It is difficult to overestimate the importance of the work begun in this direction, and I hope and believe it will be speedily crowned with success."

From GEORGE DANA BOARDMAN, D. D., of Philadelphia:

" The purpose of the Memorial Association of the District of Columbia is grateful, just, patriotic, reverent, timely, and most valuable."

From A. J. GORDON, D. D., of Boston:

"I heartily approve the purpose of the Memorial Association to preserve the historic landmarks of our capital city for the instruction and inspiration of future generations, and wish its directors all success and support."

From THOMAS S. HASTINGS, D. D., President of the Union Theological Seminary, New York:

" I have an ever-deepening affection, admiration, and reverence for that noble man whom God gave us in our time of sorest need. He is unique in my private Westminster Abbey, and I rejoice in every tribute to his memory. It would be hard for me to say whether I admire him more than I love him. At all events I am grateful to you for what you are doing to honor his memory."

From PHILIP SCHAFF, D. D., of New York:

" Your project for the preservation of the most noteworthy houses in the capital of the nation commends itself to the good judgment and taste of every patriot and lover of history."

From JOHN HALL, D. D., Pastor of the Fifth Avenue Presbyterian Church, New York:

"We are a young nation, but there are many things in the history of this great Republic, the moral influence of which on the national sentiment should be perpetuated, and it is eminently fit that the outward and sensible monuments of these things and of the men who shape the life of the United States should be nationally preserved."

From F. M. ELLIS, D. D., of Baltimore:

"I am glad for this new emphasis given by your Association to the value of objects and associations distinctly American. I congratulate the people of the national capital for the example they have thus set the country, and wish the officers of your Association the largest success."

From CHARLES S. VEDDER, D. D., Pastor of the Huguenot Church, Charleston, S. C.:

"It gives me great pleasure to know of your most laudable enterprise in rescuing the historical points of the capital city from oblivion. You have set an example which may well be followed everywhere in our cities."

From BISHOP PARET, of Maryland:

"I most warmly approve the purpose of the
Memorial Association in guarding and designating
houses and places of historic interest. I wish them
abundant success."

From BISHOP POTTER, of New York:

" The organization of the Memorial Association
of the District of Columbia was a most happy
thought, and it is fitly presided over by our honored
Chief Justice.

" It is an especial charm of foreign cities to be
able to read something of their history, and of the
men who have made them great, in ancient buildings
and landmarks; and surely no city in the world
has, during its comparatively brief life, gathered
within it more names of lasting interest and exem-
plary value, whether as citizens, statesmen, or
patriots, than Washington. I wish you all success
in your most opportune undertaking."

From BISHOP LITTLEJOHN, of Long Island:

" The Memorial Association has not, in my
judgment, been organized a day too soon. Its object is most praiseworthy and will have the cordial
approval of every patriotic citizen of our country."

From BISHOP SCARBOROUGH, of New Jersey :

" Every one who has visited Washington as a stranger, and had to gather his information from the average cab-driver about historical places in that beautiful city will appreciate the efforts of the Memorial Association. I heartily commend your unselfish work and wish you good success in it."

From BISHOP COLEMAN, of Delaware :

" The objects of the Association are such as appeal very strongly to my own sentiments and convictions. I should think they would to those of all patriotic Americans. You have my hearty wishes for the complete accomplishment of the work undertaken."

From BISHOP CLARK, of Rhode Island :

" I am glad to know that attention is beginning to be directed to the preservation of historic buildings, and I trust that the efforts of the Memorial Association will help to prevent the destruction of the few that remain. It has always seemed to me very discreditable to the city of Boston that the venerable and beautiful Hancock House was allowed to be blotted out."

From BISHOP DUDLEY, of Kentucky :

" The buildings in Washington which you propose to perpetuate and designate with appropriate inscriptions are the monuments of our national history, and better than formal obelisks will they keep alive the memory of the great events of which they were instruments. By all means should they be preserved, and I cannot doubt that the Congress will give to your Association the means to preserve them."

From BISHOP KNICKERBACKER, of Indiana:

"The objects of the Memorial Association to preserve historic buildings and mark historic places is certainly most desirable, and the generation that comes after will rise up and bless it. I hope it may succeed in all its endeavors."

From BISHOP WHIPPLE, of Minnesota:

"I heartily approve of the objects of the Memorial Association. It is our reproach that we have so little reverence for the past. Nothing can be more precious than the memorials linked with the great names of the Republic. They are silent teachers which recall the lessons of loyalty to God and to country that these men exemplified in their lives. I wish you Godspeed in your patriotic work."

From BISHOP HUNTINGTON, of Central New York:

"The purpose of the Memorial Association seems to me to be worthy, appropriate, and timely.

More so than many of the commemorative projects that are now popular."

From BISHOP LEONARD, of Ohio:

" I am greatly interested in your laudable plan. Some years back I went to Mr. W. W. Corcoran and urged him to set apart an alcove in the Art Gallery, in which might be placed prints, water-color pictures, photographs, etc., of the historic structures in and about Washington. The British Museum in London has devoted a large space to similar memorials of that ancient city, and it occurred to me that we should follow such an example. I trust that you will push this laudable enterprise till it attracts liberal attention, and I assure you of my keen interest in what you have so intelligently undertaken."

From BISHOP NEELY, of Oregon:

" I beg to assure you of my hearty commendation of the purposes of the Memorial Association, and of my hope that they may be fully realized by the co-operation of patriotic citizens."

Prom BISHOP WILLIAMS, of Connecticut:

" I can hardly imagine any better way of culti-vating that historic spirit which is so essential to the life of the nation than that which the Memorial Association has adopted. The plan has my warm interest and best wishes."

From BISHOP TUTTLE, of Missouri :

" I rejoice in the efforts you are making to fix some centres that may be sources of honest patriotic sentiment, and to preserve some shrines for patriotic devotion. My best wishes heartily go with my thanks to you and your fellow-laborers."

From BISHOP QUINTARD, of Tennessee :

"I greatly rejoice to know that such a movement has been inaugurated. I feel that it is a matter of grave interest, and that every true patriot should do his utmost for the promotion of the purposes of the organization."

From BISHOP DAVIS, of Michigan :

"Your purpose and design are such as must commend themselves to every patriotic and intelligent citizen. I wish you all success in your admirable undertaking."

From BISHOP LAWRENCE. of Massachusetts :

" Living between the Longfellow Mansion and the Washington Elm, in this old town (Cambridge), I can speak with experience and enthusiasm of the worth and interest of historic spots. Washington has before it an historic interest which no other city can claim, and the Memorial Association has a large opportunity."

From BISHOP PERRY, of Iowa :

"The preservation of the noteworthy houses at the capital as historical monuments is a matter that should elicit the approval and command the co-operation of every lover of his country. The intelligent and patriotic labors of your Association, as indicated in its charter of incorporation, will make more fair and attractive the great and glorious city which is the centre of our national life."

From BISHOP NELSON, of Georgia :

"I desire to assure you of my interest in the work of the Association. It is a startling fact that the people of our land, possessing so few antiquities, have usually been extremely careless in the preservation of those few, and I heartily indorse and approve any project which looks to the safety and custody of any links with the past, such as buildings and monuments, books and relics, which in the future, even more than at the present time, will be objects of such intense interest to our people as well as to foreigners."

From BISHOP NICHOLS, of California :

"The admirable object of the Association cannot fail to be a popular one. There is a wholesome American taste for the flavor of antiquity. We not only like to refer to the precepts of our elders, but to see where they lived and worked, and if the Association receives the attention it ought, walks

in Washington may become as picturesque of the
past as Hare's Walks in London."

From BISHOP GARRETT, of Texas:

" I am sure every patriotic citizen of the United
States must cordially approve the purpose of the
Association. Other nations cannot fail to be interested in the preservation of those monuments which
enshrine the history of great epochs in national
life. The civilized world will commend your
enterprise. The membership of your Association
is a sufficient guarantee of its sagacious and patriotic management."

From BISHOP FITZGERALD, of New York:

" The purposes of the Association are most
highly to be commended. Every earnest patriot
will wish that they may be successfully executed."

From BISHOP FOWLER, of Minneapolis:

" The Memorial Association is one that commends itself to me as a patriot. We have made
much magnificent history; it is high time we were
carefully preserving it. In every other civilized
land, and in many heathen lands, I have seen noble
monuments to their heroic dead, and the traveller
is interested in visiting the scenes that were precious in the eyes of our worthy dead. The wealth
of a country is in its heroic people; its greatness,
in the treasures it cherishes from the mighty men
of the past."

From BISHOP HAYGOOD, of Georgia :

" I hope you will accomplish the praiseworthy
ends you have in view. Few things are more important than the preservation of the memorials of
our noblest history."

From BISHOP MALLALIEU, of Buffalo :

" I most certainly commend the worthy and patriotic enterprise you have in hand. To preserve
for future generations the sites and buildings made
memorable by their association with the great and
good is to confer inspiration and blessing upon un-
counted millions. I wish you the most eminent
success."

From BISHOP WARREN, of Colorado :

" I greatly approve the work of your Association. Some of the most interesting things in Eu-
ropean cities are the places that the makers of
history have made immortal. A simple tablet
makes thousands of pilgrims stop and remember
the great deeds of great men."

From BISHOP NINDE, of Detroit :

" I shall take a warm interest in watching your
success. Our nation is ripening in age. It is be-
coming nobly historic. Its memorable places and
buildings will become shrines for the people
through the coming years to visit with increasing
interest and reverence. if they are properly marked

and preserved. I hope the praiseworthy ends of the Association will be fully realized."

From BISHOP VINCENT, of New York:

" Your objects are deserving of praise and support. I wish you success in your proposed scheme."

From BISHOP MERRILL, of Chicago:

"A good thing. Go ahead. If the list of names is an insufficient recommendation, add mine as endorsing *them*."

From BISHOP BOWMAN, of St. Louis:

"I most heartily approve of the proposed work of your Association, and trust you will be successful in accomplishing your wishes."

From BISHOP HURST, of Washington, D. C. :

"I am glad to see that a movement is begun to mark the historic houses of Washington with suitable tablets. Long since this most appropriate work should have been undertaken, and it comes now not a day too soon. Our city abounds in memorable houses, and each should be known to all the world."

48

From the Hon. CHARLES F. LIBBY, President of the Maine State Bar Association :

" While I am somewhat doubtful whether any words of mine can add weight to what has been so well put before the public by the officers of your Association, I beg to say that I heartily approve the purposes of your organization."

From the Hon. I. NEWTON FIERO, President of the New York State Bar Association :

" I beg leave to express a most earnest hope that you may be successful in procuring from Congress an appropriation sufficient for the purchase of the house in which President Lincoln died. It would certainly be most appropriate if this property should be preserved, and protected under the care of your Association. I shall take great pleasure in doing anything in my power to forward its objects."

From ALBERT CLARKE, Secretary of the Home Market Club, Boston, Massachusetts :

" Your work is of national interest and importance, and should be liberally promoted by Congress. Every historic spot in the national capital, preserved as nearly intact as possible, is an educator in patriotism, and that is the kind of education which a heterogeneous population most needs, and is in the greatest danger of neglecting. There is

no other house in Washington which I have viewed
with so great interest as the one in which Lincoln
died. This interest will be greater in others as the
event recedes. Lincoln died for his country, and
the country should help your Association to acquire
and preserve that house."

From O. L. F. BROWNE, Secretary of the
Commercial Exchange, Des Moines, Iowa :

" The following resolution has been adopted
without dissent by our Board of Managers :
" *Whereas* we believe that the object of the
Memorial Association of the District of Columbia
is a praiseworthy one, therefore, *Resolved*, by the
directors of the Commercial Exchange of Des-
Moines, Iowa, that we earnestly request that Congress make such appropriation as in its wisdom
may seem needful to the accomplishment of the
objects of the Association."

From GEORGE CLINTON, President of the
Buffalo Merchants' Exchange :

" I am decidedly of the opinion that keeping
alive and before our people the memories of our
great and good men is one of the strongest forces
that can be utilized for preserving the patriotism of
our people, and inciting the rising generation to a
generous emulation in preserving our institutions by
following in the footsteps of our illustrious statesmen. An affectionate regard for the memories of

our great leaders also requires some commemoration of their deeds. The plan of your organization I deem an excellent one, and the locality where that plan is to be carried out the most appropriate one in the United States. Congress certainly should aid you. While I have stated what I have as my personal views, yet I am sure that I reflect the feelings of the entire Merchants' Exchange."

From B. F. WHITNER, President of the State Bar Association of South Carolina :

" I need scarcely say that I most cordially commend the object and aims of your Association, as I believe every good citizen will who loves his country and is proud of its history in the march of civil and religious liberty, and of its wonderful advancement in the arts and industries of civilized life. I hope that you will receive all needed aid from Congress, and every encouragement from the people of our common country."

From CHARLES E. FLANDRAU, of St. Paul :

" I assure you, my dear sir, that I sympathize heartily with the object of your organization, and especially so as all my boyhood days were passed in the District of Columbia. I left there about 52 years ago, but have made out to return almost annually ever since, and although at one time I knew every place of interest in the whole District, I find it difficult now to locate any historical point. I will take the responsibility, without consulting the bar association, of assuring you that our sympathies are entirely with your organization, and if we can in any way aid you we will be most happy to do so."

From R. T. BARTON, Winchester, Virginia :

" I entirely sympathize with your object in marking historic houses, and especially in preserving the house in which President Lincoln died. No one who has enjoyed the pleasure which the preservation of such interesting objects in Europe affords to the traveller can fail to wish that the same thing can be accomplished in this country. I sincerely hope that Congress may be induced to make the appropriation for the purchase of this house."

From CHARLES J. SWIFT, of San Francisco :

"The purposes of the Association meet with my earnest approval."

From F. A. McWILLIE, of Jackson, Miss., Ex-President of the State Bar Association :

"The object of the Association meets my warmest approval."

From JAMES P. WINCHESTER, President of the First National Bank of Wilmington, Delaware :

"I consider the work of your Association to be most laudable. Our country needs the perpetuation of the memory of our historic men. Certainly no land has produced greater."

From DONALD FLETCHER, Banker, of Denver, Colorado :

"I have not heard of anything lately that more thoroughly pleases me than that your Association will try to have Congress purchase the house in which President Lincoln died, and mark other historic places. If I can be of any service to you command me. I assure you that every Coloradoan will heartily approve of your patriotic and thoughtful zeal."

From the Hon. E. S. LACEY, President of the Bankers' National Bank of Chicago, and lately Comptroller of the Currency :

"I note with great pleasure that the Memorial Association has been organized, and that its officers and directors are of such a character as to assure it unqualified success.

" To perpetuate and emphasize the historic interest which attaches to so many places and objects in Washington and its vicinity is a patriotic work which has been already too long delayed. The recent rapid growth of the city and the many changes now in contemplation will soon render it impossible to do this work in a satisfactory manner.

"I sincerely hope that you may be able to procure from Congress suitable appropriations for the end you have in view. The cost will be insignificant in comparison with the gratifying results which you will be able to accomplish, not only for the benefit of the present generation, but of many in the centuries to come. You have my hearty sympathy and support in your commendable efforts in this direction."

From A. BALDWIN, President of the New Orleans National Bank :

"I have read of the organization and purposes of your Association, and agree with you that it will be to the general good that these historic places should be kept and preserved."

From E. N. MORRILL, President of the First National Bank of Leavenworth, Kansas :

" I notice with pleasure your efforts to preserve and mark the noteworthy houses of the capital city, and commend most heartily your action in that direction. I have often noticed the plain brick house made historic by the death within its walls of our martyred President, and have felt that the building ought to be owned and forever preserved by our Government. I sincerely hope that Congress will at its next session make an appropriation sufficient to purchase that house, and to enable you to mark in a proper manner other buildings around which cluster many of the most sacred associations of the past."

From BRAINARD H. WARNER, President of the Washington Loan and Trust Company:

"I take pleasure in stating that I highly esteem the objects and purpose of the Association. It will doubtless serve to make known many points of great historic interest which are at present comparatively unknown."

FROM VARIOUS NEWSPAPERS.

From THE WASHINGTON POST of February 8, 1893:

"The laudable objects of the Memorial Association of the District of Columbia have been fully set forth in *The Post*, together with the names of the eighteen members of the Association, which are of themselves an all-sufficient assurance that they are governed in this matter by the utmost honesty and patriotism of purpose.

"One of the first moves of the Association, and

one that commends itself at once to public appro-
bation, is directed to the purchase of the house on
Tenth street in which Abraham Lincoln died, and
around which cluster so many melancholy associations. In the natural order of events this property
must give way to the progress of improvement, and
with it disappear one of the most memorable of all
our historic landmarks—one that possesses not only
to the citizens of Washington, but to the whole
country, a peculiarly reverent interest.

" *The Post* believes the appropriation asked for
to be meritorious and in a certain sense obligatory.
If the property is to be bought at all, instead of
being allowed to go to decay or be torn down,
it should be bought without delay, when it can be
had at a less price than it will command two years
or five years hence. It is a mansion that should be
saved as it is to future generations and cared for
with the same religious veneration that is bestowed
upon the home of Washington at Mt. Vernon.
Such, we doubt not, would be the unanimous voice
of the people, could they be heard upon this ques-
tion, and Congress need not fear the rebuke of its
constituencies for an expenditure so just and appropriate."

From the WASHINGTON STAR of October
18, 1893 :

" There are many historic structures in this city,
and these, unless either Congress or the Memorial
Association interferes, must soon decay or be re-

placed by modern dwellings. Some of these places should be saved, and if public interest can once be aroused they will be. The Association has a great task to perform, and it should receive, as it deserves, the hearty encouragement of every one whose patriotism is untainted by self-interest, and who would see this Washington of ours more beautiful and more interesting than any other city on earth. The Lincoln house and the Lincoln relics ought not, however, to be the property of an individual or an association, but of the nation. Congress ought speedily to provide for the purchase of this property, preserving with patriotic care remembrances of the great President, and honoring his name and memory."

From the INDIANAPOLIS JOURNAL of May 12, 1893:

" Of all the enterprises that present themselves from time to time for editorial comment, that which calls itself the Memorial Association of the District or Columbia seems one of the most unselfish, and unmoved by other than considerations of pure sentiment. The immediate desire of the Association is to procure from Congress an appropriation for the purchase of the house in which President Lincoln died. The object of this society, which is duly incorporated, is composed of prominent men, and has for its president Chief Justice Fuller, is highly commendable. The house in which President Lincoln died at once became a place of pilgrimage, and its associations will render it even a greater point of interest as time goes by. It should be preserved and restored by all means."

From the WYANDOTTE (Kansas) HERALD of February 2, 1893 :

" The object of the Association is a laudable one, and as the title to all property secured by it vests in the United States, Congress should not only encourage, but deal liberally and speedily with it by making such appropriations as will enable it to successfully carry out its plans and purposes."

From the NEW ORLEANS PICAYUNE of the 31st January, 1893 :

" The *Picayune* recognizes the importance of the work that the Association has undertaken to do, and wishes it all success."

From the NEW ORLEANS TIMES-DEMO-CRAT of May 22, 1893 :

" The Association will have the endorsement and good wishes of all patriotic Americans."

From the KENNEBEC (Maine) JOURNAL, February 7, 1893 :

" The rapid growth of the national capital increases the importance of the work of this organization, which has entered the field none too soon."

From the BALTIMORE NEWS. February 12, 1893:

"An organization of this kind has long been needed, and it will have the aid and sympathy of students and lovers of history as well as of the patriotic citizen."

From THE BALTIMORE SUN of May 12, 1893:

" Of the old colonial houses there are very few remaining, but the preservation of them and the marking with tablets other historic houses and places connected with the birth and earlier progress of the nation is a praiseworthy undertaking."

From THE BOSTON TRANSCRIPT of February 2, 1893:

" It is truly high time that the historic spirit had a little chance of cultivation at the national capital."

From the BOSTON TRAVELLER of February 3, 1893:

" The Memorial Association of the District of Columbia, of which Chief Justice Fuller is President, deserves the heartiest encouragement from all classes and citizens."

From the BOSTON GLOBE of September 30, 1893 :

" It is a good and patriotic undertaking ; whatever Congress can do to help it on should certainly be granted."

From the BOSTON CONGREGATIONAL-IST of October 5, 1893 :

" Such an organization was started none too soon. It is an important aid to intelligent patriotism. It should have the sympathy and support of all American citizens."

From the KANSAS CITY JOURNAL of May 12, 1893 :

" The membership of the Association includes some of the eminent men of the nation. Chief Justice Fuller being its official head. Its professed objects are most worthy, and the promoters of the movement are citizens whose character is a guarantee that its motives are pure and patriotic. It should have the encouragement and the assistance of the public and of Congress."

From THE OMAHA WORLD-HERALD of October 1, 1893 :

" Decidedly the house associated with Lincoln and many another mansion of the beautiful capital ought to be preserved. They are filled with illustrious associations."

From THE OMAHA BEE of November 5, 1893:

"The preservation of historic homes becomes a matter of national concern. Patriotic motives are strong enough to enlist a few individuals in the movement, but to conduct it properly requires the assistance of Congress. The Association relies upon the Government to come to its aid. That a building of such historic importance should belong to the people and be preserved in its original condition must be recognized by all as a praiseworthy proposition. The nation owes that much homage to the memory of the martyred President."

From THE ORANGE (New Jersey) CHRONICLE, February 4, 1893:

"Any one who has ever visited Washington keenly appreciates the need of just this thing, and will wish Godspeed to the Association in its praiseworthy efforts."

From THE ALBANY EVENING JOURNAL, February 8, 1893:

"It is hoped that Congress will see fit to further the work of the Association. The objects which it seeks to obtain are well worthy of its best efforts."

From THE NEW YORK TRIBUNE of February 9, 1893:

"A most useful and patriotic work has been undertaken by the Memorial Association of the District of Columbia. It ought not to be difficult to enlist public sympathy and the support of Congress for so noble a work. Washington has been the home for generations of great Americans who have founded and preserved national institutions, and directed the progress of a Republic that with the consent of Christendom is accounted the hope of the world. Nothing should be left undone to preserve the reminiscences of their greatness, and by memorials on every side to educate and develop the historic spirit of the coming generation."

From THE NEW YORK MAIL AND EXPRESS, Oct. 21, 1893:

" Public sentiment should speedily indicate a general desire to have the plans of the Association realized. The house in which President Lincoln died should become the property of the nation, and not remain subject to the disposition of the private owner."

From THE CINCINNATI COMMERCIAL-GAZETTE, May 13, 1893:

"A generous policy by Congress in aid of the purposes of the Memorial Association would receive the hearty endorsement of every American citizen who is proud of his country's record."

From THE PITTSBURG TIMES of May 10, 1893 :

"The Association is especially desirous of purchasing the house where President Lincoln died, which it says is the only building at the capital distinctly associated with him. The work is certainly a most commendable one, and should have the moral support of every patriotic citizen in pressing it to a speedy consummation."

From THE HOUSTON (Texas) POST of February 1, 1893 :

"It is proposed to purchase and preserve the most notable houses and mark them with suitable tablets, and thus cultivate a historic spirit, and reverence for the leaders and memories of the Republic. It is a laudable purpose, and the country and Congress should assist the Association."

From the BURLINGTON (Vermont) FREE PRESS, February 1, 1893 :

"The Memorial Association of the District of Columbia is worthy of all praise for inaugurating a movement to preserve the historic structures in and about the nation's capital, and all true Americans will rejoice that one of the first steps of the Association will be to purchase the house in that city in which the immortal Lincoln yielded up his life and restore it to the condition in which it then was."

From the JEFFERSONIAN (Piedmont, Virginia), February 7, 1893 :

" Washington being the nation's city, Congress should aid the Memorial Association of the District of Columbia in the excellent work it has undertaken."

By the REV. ROBERT P. KERR, D. D., in the RICHMOND (Virginia) TIMES, of November 9, 1893 :

" Next to religion itself there is no more elevating influence that can be brought to bear upon the rising generation than an intimate acquaintance with the lives, characters, and achievements of the great men of the country. The work of the Memorial Association will be of the greatest service in promoting patriotism and the refinements of a higher civilization, and ought to have the approval and assistance of all true Americans."

From the PARKERSBURG (West Virginia) STATE JOURNAL, January 28, 1893 :

" The first purchase by the Association will be the house in which President Lincoln died, which will belong to the United States. The movement is a most worthy one, and is especially timely in this historic and memorable year."

www.ingramcontent.com/pod-product-compliance
Lightning Source LLC
Chambersburg PA
CBHW031745090426
42739CB00008B/892